master golf

a flo

master golf

mark wood PGA Professional

A CONNECTIONS · AXIS EDITION

A Connections • Axis Edition

This edition first published in Great Britain by
Connections Book Publishing Limited
St Chad's House
148 King's Cross Road
London WC1X 9DH
and Axis Publishing Limited
8c Accommodation Road
London NW11 8ED
www.axispublishing.co.uk

Conceived and created by
Axis Publishing Limited

Creative Director: Siân Keogh
Managing Editor: Matthew Harvey
Project Designer: Zoë Dissell
Project Editor: Louise Aikman
Production Manager: Sue Bayliss
Photographer: Mike Good

Text and images copyright
© Axis Publishing Limited 2002

With thanks to 'Wilson', 'Calaway', 'Etonic Golf
Shoes', and 'Pro Quip' for their contributions
to this book.

Note
The opinions and advice expressed in this book
are intended as a guide only. The publisher and
author accept no responsibility for any injury
or loss sustained as a result of using this book.

British Library Cataloguing-in-Publication data
available on request.

ISBN 1–85906–078–1

9 8 7 6 5 4 3 2

Separation by United Graphics Pte Limited
Printed and bound by Star Standard (Pte) Limited

a *flowmotion* title

master
golf

contents

getting in shape

The perfect golf swing is full of contradictions – none of which is more important, or more baffling, than the need to focus and relax at the same time. Some golfers practise mental exercises such, as meditation, to help them achieve this difficult balancing act. The best way to start swinging a golf club is to master the technical aspects. Then you can concentrate on making a natural, fluid, swing sequence.

The first thing to learn to aquire a good golf swing is the correct posture. Many golf professionals stress that the proper stance makes all the difference between a good and a bad swing. The swing should be a natural movement of the body, during which the clubhead happens to make contact with the ball. The correct starting position is therefore essential if you want to swing the club properly..

addressing the ball

The set-up before a shot is critical for the angles you create at this point ultimately dictate the line along which the club is swung. If you stand over the ball incorrectly, you will swing along the wrong line and end up hitting a bad shot. To address the ball properly: first, stand tall and upright; next, bend the knees slightly, so that your body weight moves to the balls of the feet; stick your backside

THE STANCE Getting into the proper stance for a golf shot should be a natural movement. Bend the knees first, stick your backside out, keep your spine straight and lean over the ball. Let your hands hang down naturally. You will now be in the correct position. It is worth using a drill like this to get into position before you start your swings.

out, keeping your spine as straight as possible; keep your chin clear of your chest, so that your shoulders can rotate easily underneath your head; let your arms hang down naturally, directly in front of you. Your hands should be now 6–7 inches away from your left thigh. Position the feet a shoulder-width gap apart between the inside part of the heels. The toes should be pointing outwards slightly.

The leading arm (the arm closest to the target – the left for right-handed players) should be comfortably straight, but not tense. The rear elbow (the one furthest from the target – the right for right-handed players) should be relaxed with the point of the elbow pointing towards your rear hip. Move your hands slightly towards the target. Your hands should be in line with the front part of the ball.

Your leading eye should try to look at the back of the ball. A handy tip is to position the ball so that the maker's name is just visible at the rear of the golf ball looked at with your left eye. From the side, a line drawn from your shoulders down should fall through the front of your knees to the middle part of your feet.

This is the basic stance for all golf shots. From this position you will be able to launch good, accurate golf swings. Although the ball position may change when using different clubs, the basic posture remains the same. When practising, focus on making the swing a flowing movement, moving from the hips and shoulders. Remember not to focus on the ball.

ALIGNMENT For a standard shot, a line drawn between your toes should run in the direction of the target. The face of the club should be facing the same direction. Combined, the two lines form a track running straight to the target.

the grip

The grip is the interface between you and the golf club. You need to hold the club in such a way that you can complete a full swing, turn your wrists at the appropriate moments, and have complete control over the orientation of the clubface. A number of different techniques have been developed over the years, and it is largely a matter of trial and error to find the one that suits you. There are three principal grips to choose between: the overlapping grip (also known as the Vardon grip); the interlocking grip and the baseball grip. Each has its own advantages and disadvantages and each suits different types of player. The grip for the leading hand is nearly always the same: it is the manner in which the rear hand connects with the leading hand that varies. To adopt the proper grip with your left hand, simply hang your arms by your side and have someone place a club in your left hand. The natural grip that you will need to grasp the club is the basis of the golf grip. The left thumb should be placed down the shaft, just to the right of centre. The shaft should run across the base of your last three fingers and across the middle part of the index finger.

THE OVERLAPPING GRIP

Also known as the Vardon grip, after the famous British golfer, Harry Vardon, who used it, the overlapping grip involves placing the little finger of the rear hand over the gap between the index finger and forefinger of the leading hand. This is the most popular grip among professional golfers.

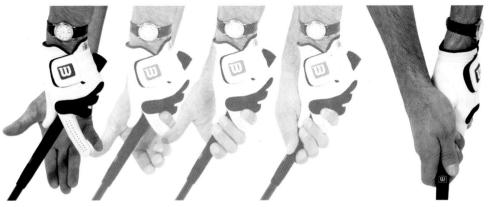

THE INTERLOCKING GRIP

This grip is similar to the overlapping grip, but in this case the little finger of the leading hand and the index finger of the rear hand actually hook together. Otherwise, the grip is the same. Players with small hands, such as Jack Nicklaus, find this grip more comfortable. For the same reason, many women players also use the interlocking grip.

THE BASEBALL GRIP

Also known as the 'ten-fingered grip', this position involves holding the grip with all 10 fingers. This grip is predominantly used by juniors or people with small or weak hands. First wrap the fingers of the leading hand around the grip, then tuck the fingers of the rear hand just below. The fingers should not interlock, but the index finger of the leading hand should touch the little finger of the rear hand. Controlling the clubhead is more difficult with this grip as more 'cocking' of the hands occurs.

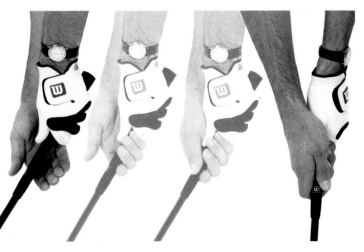

basic swing

The key to a good swing is to make a rotational action with your shoulders, hips and wrists. The leading side of the body controls the backswing, while the rear side of the body controls the downswing.

When you take the clubhead away from the ball at the start of the swing, try to move the shoulders, arms and club away as a one-piece unit. The left shoulder, left knee and arms should all move together. The clubhead should be drawn away from the ball for the first 12–18 inches in a straight line. When it reaches waist height position, the left arm should still be extended with the club set behind the body. As the chest and shoulders continue to rotate, the arms can move up, reaching the top of the backswing position. The shoulders have now turned at 90 degrees to the ball. The hips are turned to 45 degrees and the body weight is transferred from the leading to the rear side of the body. The rear leg should be firm, supporting that weight. Although you are transferring weight to the rear side by rotating, you are not moving laterally, only pivoting.

GETTING THE RHYTHM
It is crucial to make sure that you stand over the ball in a relaxed position before the swing. Any tension will only impede the fluidity of your turning action and the rhythm of your swing. If you hold the club too tight, the muscles in your hand will tense and this will stop the wrist from turning and squaring the clubhead up with the ball. For the wrist action, imagine you are cracking a whip – the wrist is allowed to flick, thus creating more clubhead speed when hitting through the ball.

The start of the downswing is initiated by the lower part of the body – the hips and legs. This action has a pulling effect on the arms and the upper body. Look at the club at waist height position in the backswing, with the wrists cocked and hinged. Compare this with the equivalent position on the downswing. The downswing is on a slightly flatter arc attacking the ball. By moving the lower part of the body first, you are creating a slingshot effect with the upper body, arms and club. With the club at waist height the rear forearm and wrist make a downward blow into the ground behind the back of the ball. As the forearm is making this downward blow, the wrist rotates the clubface back to a square position for impact. The rear side of the body now starts to rotate round with the clubhead. The rear knee rotates at the same time as the clubhead, the triangle of the arms, hand and club keeps rotating through the ball.

shoulder & hip exercises

If you ask someone who has never picked up a golf club to hit a ball, you can imagine the sort of swing that would result. Newcomers are likely to hold the club in their rear hand, bend their knees, raise the club without any movement of the shoulders and strike at the ball with a movement of the arm similar to skimming a stone across water. There would be lots of wrist movement, the elbow would be waving all over the place – and they would probably miss the ball. To encourage your shoulders and not the arms to drive the swing, try using the exercise below. Adopt the posture

for a golf swing (see pages 4–5). Instead of letting your hands hang down in front of you, hold a club against your shoulders with your fingertips, arms crossed over your sternum. Keeping the arms locked in place, play an imaginary golf shot. First, turn the shoulders so that the end of the golf club is pointing in front of your left foot. Now, rotate the shoulders through the downswing and follow through, keeping the shaft locked against your shoulders. This will help to reduce the tendency to overuse your arms in your swing.

TURNING THE SHOULDERS

The other power house of the golf swing is the hips. Achieving the proper rotation of the hips and shift of weight between one side of the body and the other makes the difference between good and bad golfers. Use this exercise to get your hips rotating – something you might not have done since you last visited a nightclub. Start in the correct posture for a golf swing, but hold the club with both your hands on the shaft. Position your hands so that they are resting on your waist. Now perform the motion of a golf swing. On the backswing, try to get the club as close to 90 degrees from its starting position as possible (without straining). Keep your shoulders in line with your hips and move your weight onto the rear leg. Now continue into the downswing. Rotate your hips until they you are pointing in the direction of your imaginary shot. As you turn through the ball, your weight shifts onto the front foot and your rear leg bends at the knee. All the way through the exercise, the club should be held in place at your waist. This will exaggerate the movement of the hips and help you to see the amount of movement that you are managing to make.

TURNING THE HIPS

clubs

The basic golf set consists of woods, numbered from 1 to 5, and irons, numbered from 3 to the various wedges. There are also 1- and 2-irons, although these are rarely used. The irons are designed to achieve certain trajectories and distances, while the woods are the long hitters with varying degrees of loft. Putters are designed for playing the ball on the green. There are many designs and it is largely a matter of personal choice.

Golfers are allowed to carry 14 clubs in their bag at one time. Most choose to carry a driver, a 3-wood, a putter and irons 3 to 9. This leaves five other clubs to select. Many golfers choose to carry three utility wedges and at least one lofted wood, but it is purely a matter of personal choice.

DISTANCES Irons range from 2- to 9-iron. Each iron produces a different lofting angle – the face of the 2-iron is angled at 18 degrees, and the angle increases by 4 degrees for each higher numbered iron. The shaft also reduces in length as the club number increases, requiring a slightly higher swing plane. Woods are numbered 1 to 5. The lower clubs send the ball further, although they don't lift the ball as much as the higher numbered clubs. The sand wedge usually has the highest trajectory, with a clubface angle of 58 degrees.

AVERAGE DISTANCES

CLUB	MEN	WOMEN	CLUB	MEN	WOMEN
DRIVER	230 yards	200 yards	5-IRON	160 yards	140 yards
3-WOOD	210 yards	180 yards	6-IRON	150 yards	130 yards
4-WOOD	200 yards	170 yards	7-IRON	140 yards	120 yards
5-WOOD	180 yards	160 yards	8-IRON	130 yards	110 yards
2-IRON	190 yards	170 yards	9-IRON	120 yards	100 yards
3-IRON	180 yards	160 yards	PITCHING WEDGE	110 yards	90 yards
4-IRON	170 yards	150 yards	SAND WEDGE	90 yards	80 yards

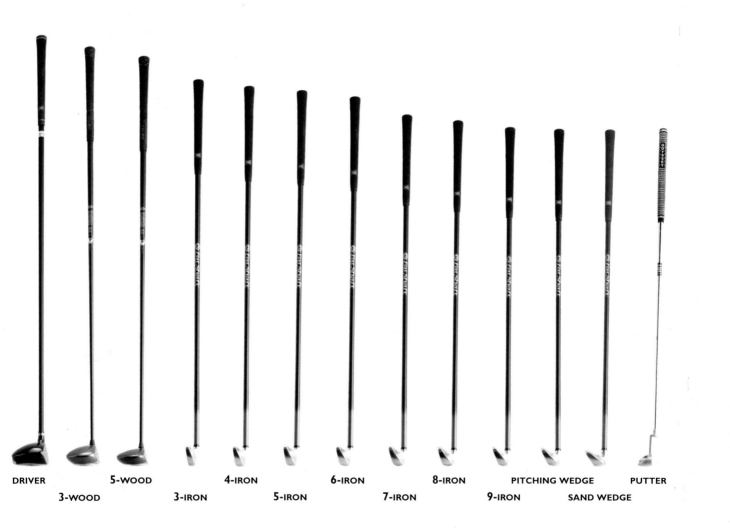

DRIVER

3-WOOD

5-WOOD

3-IRON

4-IRON

5-IRON

6-IRON

7-IRON

8-IRON

9-IRON

PITCHING WEDGE

SAND WEDGE

PUTTER

shoes, gloves & waterproofs

The type of clothing you wear to play golf can sometimes depend on the regulations or norms of a particular golf course. If you're unsure about the dress code, it is easy to give the professional's shop a call to find out. Usually, most golf courses simply have regulations discouraging the wearing of jeans, and insist that you wear suitable shoes. However, the crucial aspect to remember when choosing clothing is to avoid tight items – as this can affect your swing.

shoes

The most important part of a golfer's shoe is the sole. Whether you choose to have spikes or not should depend on the type of golf course you are playing on. Don't forget, you can always bring two pairs and alternate depending on the terrain. Spikes help your shoe grip the ground, giving your swing a stable base. They are particularly helpful when negotiating a hilly course. The traditional metal spikes associated with the early days of golf have been replaced with a whole range of soft spike alternatives. The bonus of this modern initiative is twofold. Firstly, and perhaps most importantly, soft spikes are much more comfortable to wear for long period of times. Secondly, these soft spikes provide much better protection for the green, allowing you to enjoy a smooth game. Non-spiked shoes have the advantage of being a lot lighter and are therefore more suitable for hard fairways.

UMBRELLA Golf umbrellas are useful for keeping your club handles dry. They are particularly effective in heavy showers but may be problematical in windy weather due to their large size. Never use an umbrella when lightning is likely.

SPIKES You can buy different spikes depending on the weather conditions. Below are examples of the heavier ones that are suitable for rainy, wintery weather, and the lighter plastic ones that are worn in warmer conditions.

SHOES The major factor in deciding which type of shoe to wear is whether to have spikes or not. Spiked shoes are particularly suitable for a hilly course and can help your grip if you are playing in wet conditions. Non-spiked shoes perform best on hard fairways.

GLOVES A glove is worn on your leading hand to help it remain firm and not slip as you play your shot. Some gloves include instructions concerning fitting advice and it is best to follow this advice closely, as the wrong fit can affect your swing.

gloves and waterproofs

A glove can really assist with your grip at the top of the shaft – and reduces the risk of blisters. There is a huge range of gloves on the market made from both leather and synthetic material. When choosing gloves it s essential to find ones that fit properly – if they are too tight they can affect your circulation and will encumber your shot. This advice also applies when choosing waterproof items of clothing. Make sure your waterproofs are not too tight fitting – especially across the shoulders. It is also advisable to buy light-weight waterproofs that let the perspiration escape and keep your body temperature even.

rules and etiquette

The basic rules and etiquette of golf are simple. They are based on consideration for your fellow players and on ensuring that the game runs as smoothly as possible for everyone concerned. The rules can get overcomplicated in competition situations, but the basic principles involve playing the course as you find it, playing the ball as it lies and following the rules when you can't do either of these.

different tees

Most golf courses have three levels of teeing area at each hole. The closest to the hole is normally used by women, the middle one by men and the furthest one for competitions. Some courses have a fourth tee area for championship-level play. Make sure that you tee off from the correct area.

congestion

If you have lost your ball and cannot find it within five minutes, allow others to play on. Wait until all players have finished and are out of range before playing on.

bunkers

Make sure that you don't touch the sand with the clubhead at address. You should always rake over the sand after playing out of a bunker.

during play

Once a player starts to address the ball, no one should move, talk, or stand too close to that player or the hole. It is the responsibility of players and onlookers to avoid accidents caused by distraction.

the green

This is the most vulnerable part of the golf course. If you displace any turf during play it is important that any damage is repaired immediately so that other players aren't affected. You also need to make sure that any holes and footprints made to the green are smoothed over. Pitchmarks (impressions caused by the impact of a golf ball) can be repaired with special tools (below) and then the ground levelled using a putter. Leave all

PITCHMARKS When your ball lands on the green it can leave a pitchmark. Repair these using specially designed tools (left) that lever the ground back into shape. At the far left is a ball marker for use on the green.

clubs and trolleys off the putting surface once on the green, you are allowed to pick up your ball to clean it, or if it is impeding the shots of other players, marking its exact position with a ball marker (below, left).

obstructions

Natural objects such as trees and bushes are regarded as hazards – you must either play around them or take a one-shot penalty. If you cannot play your ball where it lies (if it has landed in deep water, for example), you have one of three options. First, you can play from where you hit your last shot. Second, you can drop the ball within two club lengths of where the ball is, but no closer to the hole. Third, drop your ball at any point behind you on the line formed between your present position and the hole. Objects of nature, such as leaves, are considered impediments and can be moved. Man-made objects that can be moved, such as rakes or litter, can be removed without a penalty. If a fixed man-made object, such as a tree support, bench or litter bin, obstructs your stance or your swing you can drop the ball in a more accessible position. To do this, find the nearest spot to your ball's position where it is possible to take a shot. Mark this spot with a tee and measure a club's length from the tee. Any place within a club length of the mark is appropriate for dropping the ball – but not nearer the hole. Drop the ball from an upright position with your arm outstretched, and make sure that the ball doesn't fall any closer to the pin.

PENALTIES

If you play in front of the tee marker you incur a two-stroke penalty in strokeplay.

If you tee off from the wrong ground, you are liable for a penalty and this varies depending on which type of game you are playing. If you tee off from the wrong ground and do not correct your mistake then you may be disqualified.

In a bunker, touching the sand with your clubhead when you address the ball incurs a penalty.

If the ball moves after you have addressed it (except on the tee), you will receive a one-stroke penalty. Note that you need to be aware that you are the only judge of whether your ball is playable or not, so it is up to you to decide before your shot whether to continue to play or accept a penalty.

If your partner or caddie touch the putting green to indicate the line of a putt you will be immediately penalised.

handicap and game variations

working out your handicap

The handicap system allows for players of different abilities to play a competitive game of golf together. In fact it isn't a handicap system – it's an advantage system. The principle of the system is that less able players are given a head start over better players. You need to play 10 rounds over 18 holes to work out your handicap for the first time. If you have played more than 10 rounds, you take the best 10 of the most recent 20 rounds. Work out the average score. If your average works out at 95 shots to get round 18 holes, then you will have a handicap of 20 on a par 75 course. So your handicap is the number of shots over par that you normally take to complete 18 holes. This number is then taken away from your final score. So if you scored 93 on a par 75 course, your adjusted score would be 73. This would beat someone with a handicap of ten who scored 90 (their adjusted score would end up as 80).

variations on the game

The basic object of a game of golf is to get around the course in the least number of shots. However, there are a number of ways that this basic structure can be adapted. In competitions, two basic scoring systems are used. The stableford system involves adding up scores for each hole. For example, if you hit one under par, you score three, if you make par you score two and if hit one over par you score one. If you hit more than one over par, then you score zero. This means that you don't have to complete every hole – if you hit too many shots you can simply move onto the next hole. The other common system, known as medal, uses strokeplay to make scores. This involves adding up the number of strokes taken over the course. This is the most common system used by non-competition golfers. Finally, match play involves playing your opponent for each hole. You can either win, lose or halve (draw) each hole. The one with the most wins at the end of the round is the overall winner. This system is often used when large teams play each other, for example the Ryder Cup competition between Europe and America.

Within the basic parameters of scoring, there are various ways in which the game can be structured. Foursomes is a game in which two teams of two players compete, each team using just one ball each. Each player in the team plays alternate strokes.

'Best ball' is also a team game – usually made up of two teams of two. This time, the players hit a ball each round the course, but at the end of each hole, only the best score of each team is added to total.

Another interesting golf variation is 'greensomes'. This game is also made up of teams of two players. This time, each player drives off from the tee. Each team then plays the best drive. From this point, the players alternate shots until the end of the hole. In these type of matches, handicaps cannot be used to adjust the scores.

go with the flow

The special Flowmotion images used in this book have been created to ensure that you see the whole of each swing – not just selected highlights. Each of the image sequences flows across the page from left to right, demonstrating how the swing progresses and how to achieve a smooth transition through each stage of the swing. The captions along the bottom of the images provide additional useful information to help you perform your golf swing confidently and to help you enhance your game overall. Below this, another layer of information is contained in the timeline, including indications of the various stages of the swing and symbols indicating when to hold a position. Combined, these various levels of information will help you to achieve flowing and effective golf swings – and so help you become a better golfer.

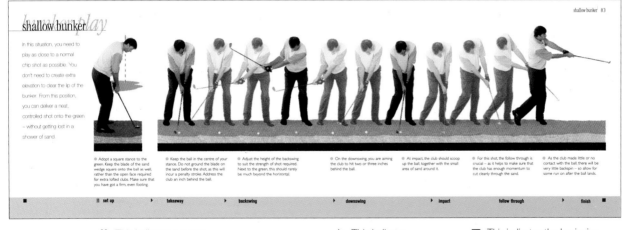

shallow bunker play

shallow bunker 83

In this situation, you need to play as close to a normal chip shot as possible. You don't need to create extra elevation to clear the lip of the bunker. From this position, you can deliver a neat, controlled shot onto the green – without getting lost in a shower of sand.

○ Adopt a square stance to the green. Keep the blade of the sand wedge square onto the ball as well, rather than the open face required for extra lofted clubs. Make sure that you have got a firm, even footing.

○ Keep the ball in the centre of your stance. Do not ground the blade on the sand before the shot, as this will incur a penalty stroke. Address the club an inch behind the ball.

○ Adjust the height of the backswing to suit the strength of shot required. Next to the green, this should rarely be much beyond the horizontal.

○ On the downswing, you are aiming the club to hit two or three inches behind the ball.

○ At impact, the club should scoop up the ball, together with the small area of sand around it.

○ For this shot, the follow through is crucial – as it helps to make sure that the club has enough momentum to cut cleanly through the sand.

○ As the club made little or no contact with the ball, there will be very little backspin – so allow for some run on after the ball lands.

■ | ‖ set up | ▶ takeaway | ▶ backswing | ▶ downswing | ▶ impact | follow through | ▶ finish ■

‖ This indicates a pause, where you should hold a position for a moment.

▶ This indicates continued movement in the sequence.

■ This indicates the beginning or end of a sequence, where there is no movement.

tee shots

driver — 1-wood

It is crucial that you can rely on a consistent swing for your big guns.

Small improvements to the swing can add yards to your drive.

● Address the ball. Run through a few checks. The angle of the club from the ground should be about 45 degrees, the ball should be about in line with the heel of your left foot and your feet a shoulder-width apart.

● Keep the movement away from the ball low and slow. The elbows should remain fixed at this point. Weight starts to shift onto the right foot and the waist begins to flex around with the shoulders.

● As your left arm reaches horizontal, the right elbow begins to bend. The waist continues to coil, shifting weight onto your back foot as your front knee bends inwards. Remember to keep your eye on the ball throughout.

● At the top of the backswing, your shoulders should have turned away from the target. The downswing is actually an uncoiling of your body. This should happen from the ground up, starting with your front knee.

● The front knee moves forward until it is over the front foot. Next, your front hip moves forward until it is over your front knee and foot. The shoulders, arms, wrists and, of course, club follow the uncoiling motion.

● The right arm straightens as the club passes horizontal again. The final uncoiling is that of the wrists. At the point of contact, the leading shoulder is raised above the following one.

● The motion of the swing continues through and the body coils in the other direction. Don't lift your eyes from the ground until your body twists to face the target direction.

▶ **downswing**   ▶ **impact**   **follow through**   ▶ **finish** ■

3-wood tee shots

There are many situations where a 3-wood is preferable to a 1-wood. It provides added control in difficult weather conditions and enables more accurate ball placement than a 1-wood.

- Address the ball, with the club at a slightly steeper angle than with the 1-wood. The idea with woods is to sweep up through the ball, rather than down onto the ball as with irons.

- The distance between the legs is shoulder-width, with the front foot pointing towards 10 o'clock and the back foot towards 1 o'clock (if 12 o'clock is straight in front of you).

- The angle of your head is defined by your relation to the ball. Try to keep the ball in the centre of your field of vision. This will prevent you from looking too far down or up.

- Keep the ball in the centre of your field of vision until the end of the follow through. This will help to keep the rest of your body in line for the entire swing.

● At the top of the backswing, your body is totally coiled, ready to unravel and deliver all its power onto the club head and so onto the ball. Remember, it's your whole body that drives the ball away, not just your arms.

● Don't focus too much on the point of impact itself. Think of trying to make the whole shape of the swing as perfect as possible. This will help to ensure that you strike the ball well.

● The follow through is just as important a part of the swing as the backswing and downswing. If you focus on making this stage tidy, you will help to keep everything that comes before it tidy and the impact will be clean.

● Allow your head to lift only when your arms and shoulders have rotated you face the target. Keep the centre of rotation around the front hip and leg – don't sway forward.

▶ **downswing**　　　▶ **impact**　　　**follow through**　　▶ **finish**　■

1-iron *tee shots*

The 1-iron is a useful club, but requires some expertise to master. It can be used instead of a driver when you need more distance than the 3-wood offers, but more accuracy than the 1-wood. It is less lofty than the 3-wood, giving the ball a shallower trajectory. The ball will therefore hit the ground at a greater speed and will run on further.

A steady swing is crucial for effective use of the 1-iron.

● Position the ball towards the front of your stance, in line with the inside heel of your leading foot.

● Take the club away from the ball as long and as low as possible, before moving into the upper backswing.

● Moving your weight onto the rear side of your body, turn the waist and shoulders round until they are facing away from the target.

● Lean into the downswing slightly, leading with your knees and uncoiling the rest of your body at the ball.

● Strike up at the ball. The 1-iron can be an unforgiving club, so be sure to connect the sweet spot of the clubface with the ball. A good impact will be rewarded with a long and accurate shot.

● Continue to transfer weight onto the leading side of the body in the follow through, pivoting on your leading hip and leg.

● End the swing facing the direction of the target. Your weight should be fully transferred forward – almost as if you were about step forward.

▶ **downswing**   ▶ **impact**   **follow through**   ▶ **finish** ■

3- & 4-iron

For par 3 holes, you can take advantage of the increased
accuracy and control of the middle irons.

● The angle of the club is steeper
than with the woods. The knees are
flexed more and your head should be
further over the ball.

● The ball should lie further towards
your back foot than when using the
woods. Line it up slightly inside the
heel of your front foot, but still not
quite central between the feet.

● The reason for the change of
stance is that the action of the swing
will be to chop down onto the ball,
not to sweep up through it as with
the woods. By having the ball further
back, the impact is earlier in the swing.

● At the top of the swing you should
be very nearly looking directly down
onto the ball over your leading
shoulder. The plane of the swing is
slightly steeper than that of the wood
swing.

■   set up   ▶   takeaway   ▶   backswing

● On the downswing, allow your body to uncoil from the ground up. Straighten your wrists to create the final push to clubhead.

● At impact, your rear leg is bent at the knee as your body twists on the front hip and leg.

● The rear leg is dragged onto its toes as you continue into the follow through. The head is still looking down at this point, keeping the body pinned down, neat and focused.

● At the end of the swing, all of your weight should have moved onto your front foot and your waist and shoulders should be facing the direction of the target (and, hopefully, that of the ball).

▶ **downswing**　　　▶ **impact**　　　**follow through**　　　▶ **finish**　　■

5- & 6-iron

The smaller the club you can use for a shot, the better. The shorter irons give you accuracy – both in terms of where the ball lands and how much it runs.

● As the clubs get shorter, the placing of the ball in relation to your feet moves towards the centre of your stance. With the 5- and 6-irons, the ball is slightly more central than with the 3 and the 4.

● If you want the accuracy of a mid or short iron, but need a little extra distance, try placing the ball about an inch further back than normal. This will effectively change the face of the club to the angle of a longer club.

● Another method of adding a few extra yards is to speed up the downswing. As you gain in experience, you will find that your normal swing leaves a reserve of power and speed for use in special situations.

● Golf pros have noticed that a ball that draws (curves from the right to left for a right-handed player) tends to travel further when it lands. Therefore creating a drawing spin on the ball can help to create a bit more distance.

● To create draw, place the ball a little further back and align your body slightly to the right (front shoulder towards the ball). As the club hits the ball it will spin it to the side and cause it to curve as it flies.

● In the same way that a draw adds distance, a fade (where the ball curves from left to right for a right-handed player) will shorten the shot. You can achieve a controlled fade using the opposite of the draw technique.

● To create fade, position the ball slightly forward of its normal position. Line the club up so that it faces the target, but align your body slightly to the left (front shoulder away from the ball). Hit the ball as normal.

▶ **downswing**　　　　　▶ **impact**　　　　　**follow through**　　　　　▶ **finish** ■

7- & 8-iron

Even when you use an iron from the tee, always tee up the ball, the advantage gained makes for a cleaner strike and more power is delivered to the ball. This not only adds distance, but also aids the accurate placement of the shot. So if you can, use a tee.

● The higher the number, the shorter the shaft of the club and the steeper the angle between the club and the ground. With your stance the head is now nearly directly over the ball.

● One of the keys to any swing is the transfer of weight between the front and back leg. At the set up, you should aim to have 60 per cent of your weight on the rear side (the side away from the target).

● As the backswing progresses, the rear knee straightens but should retain some flex. This will help provide both power and accuracy to the swing. Your weight has now shifted to the inside of your rear knee.

● As the body uncoils, weight shifts through the knees to the front leg. The body moves towards the target until the front knee, hip and foot are in line. From this point, continue to uncoil around the left hip and leg.

● Keep the downswing smooth and steady, don't rush things. As you gain experience, you will find you can add speed to the swing when you need extra distance, without losing your smooth, flowing action.

● Continue the transfer of weight into the follow through. Your front foot should now be carrying nearly all your weight. The rear foot is merely helping your balance.

● Avoid the temptation to step forward with your rear foot at the end of the swing. This can cause you to move weight off the rear foot too early and so reduce the power and accuracy of the shot.

▶ **downswing**   ▶ **impact**   **follow through**   ▶ **finish** ■

9-iron & pitching wedge

On rare occasions, you might need to use a 9-iron or pitching wedge for a tee shot. In very poor weather, for a short par 3 or to avoid excessive run-on you will need the ultra control and accuracy of the short irons.

● Many professionals say the key to a good shot is to visualize the intended journey of the ball. Step behind the ball and pick a distant target to aim for – a tree or a bunker for example. This will be your direction guide.

● As you address the ball, visualize the ball travelling towards the chosen target. Ignore any obstacles on either side, just see your ball flying straight towards the target.

● At the top of the backswing, the plane of the swing is more upright than with the longer clubs. As a result of this steeper arc, you will be hitting down onto the back of the ball, generating backspin.

● As you start the downswing, keep visualizing the target and the flight of the ball. Once you have a few games under your belt, the swing will take care of itself.

● Don't focus too much on the impact with the ball. If the whole of the swing is steady and well-timed, then the impact with the ball will also be nice and solid.

● After impact, avoid the temptation to look up quickly and check whether your shot has lived up to your visualization. Let your head rise naturally with the follow-through.

● You should end the swing facing the direction of the target. Hopefully, your ball will already be on its way there.

▶ **downswing**   ▶ **impact**   **follow through**   ▶ **finish** ■

shots from the fairway

3-wood

On a long par 4 or par 5 hole,
your second shot will have to
travel almost as far as your
drive. If the lie of the ball
is good, you will be
able to use a 3- or a
5-wood to put some
power into your shot.

● Carefully check the lie of your ball. If the approach of the swing is obstructed at all, you will need to switch to an iron for your shot. For wood fairway shots, the ball should be easily accessible.

● Settle the clubhead next to the ball as you set up. If the clubface cannot rest in line with the ball, then you should consider using an iron for the shot.

● Your swing for the fairway shot should be slightly less powerful than the tee shot with the 3-wood. Instead, you should be focusing on controlling the shot and making sure you establish good contact with the ball.

● On the downswing, keep the wrists cocked until the leading arm comes down almost in line with the ball. Once this happens, release your wrists.

● Remember that the ball hit by the 3-wood will not have any backspin. This means you can't aim to land on the green – the ball will just run on.

● If you do plan to reach the green, land the ball short of the target so that the ball will run-on towards the flag and give your shot more legs.

● As control is so important for this shot, make sure you follow through properly. This will help to guarantee a good, clean impact with the ball.

▶ **downswing**　　　　▶ **impact**　　　　**follow through**　　　▶ **finish**　　■

5-wood

With a good lie and over 150 yards to go to the green, the 5-wood will give you a good compromise between distance and control.

● Although it is easier to control than the 3-wood, you should still make sure that the lie of your ball is suitable for a wood shot. If you are lucky, the grass may have given your ball a natural tee.

● Line the ball up just inside the heel of the front foot. As you set up the shot, check that the clubface has good access to the ball and that your stance is good. Don't be afraid to change to an iron, even at this late stage.

● Once you have committed to a shot and begun the takeaway, you should be completely focused on the swing. Visualizing the shot, the flight of the ball and the intended target will help you to keep your focus sharp.

● The challenge with a wood shot off the fairway is to control the power of the shot and the impact with the ball. Keep your eye on the ball as you reach the top of the backswing.

● Keep the wrists cocked until the momentum of the swing naturally snaps them straight.

● Sweep the clubface up through the ball. It can be difficult to get a good, clean contact with the ball with a wood on the fairway, so concentrate on keeping your swing smooth and consistent.

● The trajectory of your shot will be lower than with a tee shot with a 5-wood. This means it will be shorter, but will have more run when it lands.

● Check the position of your body as you finish the shot. If you are in an incorrect position here, it is likely that something has gone wrong earlier on in the swing. Trace the problem back.

▶ **downswing**   ▶ **impact**   **follow through**   ▶ **finish** ◼

3- & 4-iron shots

The 3- and the 4-irons are probably the most popular clubs for the fairway. They provide good distance while also giving you more control over the ball than any of the woods.

● Settle into your stance as you address the ball. Line the ball up about an inch inside the heel of your leading foot. As you might have just used a wood for your drive, spend a few seconds checking your stance.

● Irons generate more backspin on the ball than the woods. This means you can aim closer to the green and count on less run-on.

● Remember that the trajectory of the ball will be slightly lower than if you had used a tee for the shot.

● As you take the club away from the ball, keep your arms and shoulders forming a triangle, until the right elbow breaks to guide the club into the top of the backswing.

● At the top of the backswing, the leading shoulder should be behind the ball. Now your body is fully coiled and ready to deliver controlled impact to the ball.

● Uncoil from the feet. The wrists should be the last to straighten up. This gradual uncoiling delivers the maximum power to the clubhead.

● Just because you are on the fairway instead of the tee, you still have to observe the basics of a good swing. This includes the follow through – often neglected, but an essential part of any golf shot.

● Pause a moment before breaking the final posture of the swing. This will effectively bookend the sequence.

▶ **downswing**   ▶ **impact**   **follow through**   ▶ **finish** ■

5-, 6- & 7-iron shots

The closer you get to the pin, the more accuracy becomes your prime objective. For shots that are too long for pitching or chipping, but too close for a long iron or wood, the 5-, 6- and 7-irons come into play. Now is the time to really start focusing in on that pin. Visualization is all important at this stage.

● Line the ball between the heel of your leading foot and the central point between both feet. This position, further back than with the longer irons, enables you to bring the club down onto the ball.

● Your head is further over the ball than with the longer clubs. Remember to keep your right knee flexed as you proceed through the backswing. This will give more power to your shot.

● If you are worried about lofting the ball too much with these clubs, try moving a bit of weight onto the leading foot as you set up. This should help to keep the ball down.

● The action of the wrists is all-important. Make sure that they remain cocked until the last stages of your downswing. Also, remember the right knee – this should be giving power to the swing at this point.

● Depending on where you have positioned yourself in relation to the ball, you will impact as the club is still on its downswing, or at the very bottom of the swing.

● Turn your shoulders through the ball and on to face the direction of the target. Your weight transfers smoothly from the rear hip onto the leading hip.

● Keep your head down until the movement of your shoulders and waist brings it up naturally.

▶ **downswing**   ▶ **impact**   **follow through**   ▶ **finish** ■

short irons – the approach shots

When the pin comes within 140 yards, it's time to bring out the short irons. They give you the most control and accuracy of all of the clubs (excluding the putter). Depending on your ability, the 8-iron can still cover up to 150 yards.

● Take some time to get your stance right for this shot. Position the ball centrally between your feet. Your feet should be slightly closer together than with the longer irons and woods.

● The plane of the swing is more upright than those of the longer clubs. You should start the shot looking down onto the ball.

● For most approach shots you will use a three-quarter backswing. This will enhance the control you have over the shot – you can add more power where necessary.

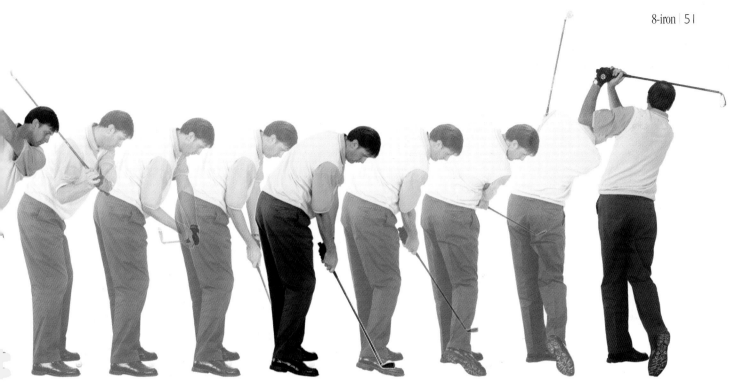

● With the weight on the balls of your feet, you will have much more room to swing your shoulders and arms in this upright position.

● From the 5-iron up to the sand wedge, a full swing will put backspin on the ball. This is because of the flatter angle at which the face of those clubs hits the ball.

● Backspin will enable you to place the ball much more accurately. You can count on the ball stopping within a few yards of where it lands.

● The height of the trajectory with the short irons also means that the ball does not travel as far when it lands.

▶ **downswing**   ▶ **impact**   **follow through**   ▶ **finish** ■

9-iron

The 9-iron is the loftiest club
before the wedges. It can still
hit the ball some 130 yards,
but is very versatile for short
approach shots of around
100 yards. As you reach
the shortest irons, you'll need
to make a few changes to
your stance and set up.

● Your stance should be slightly
narrower than with the longer irons
(feet closer together). Also, open your
stance slightly by bringing your leading
foot back an inch.

● Position the ball between the
central point of your feet and the heel
of your rear foot.

● As the backswing proceeds, flex the
wrists so that the shaft of the club is
pointing at a 40 degree angle.

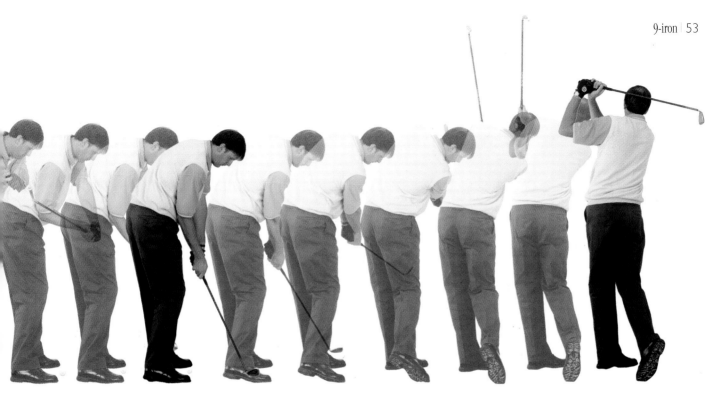

● Don't release the wrists from their position until late in the downswing. Your hands remain passive throughout.

● The clubface digs the ball out and squeezes it forward. The nearly upright angle of the club means that the action is to chop down onto the ball, not to sweep up through it as with the woods.

● Turn your upper body through the ball and on to face the direction of the target.

● The club comes up in front of the leading shoulder at a much steeper angle than with the lower irons and the woods.

▶ **downswing**   ▶ **impact**   **follow through**   ▶ **finish**   ■

pitching wedge shots

It can be tempting when using the pitching wedge to swing your wrists more than usual in order to lift the ball. The face of the club will do this for you, so stick to your normal swing routine.

● If you find yourself using too much wrist when using the lofty clubs, try sliding a pen under the face of your watch. This will act as a splint, keeping the crucial leading wrist from breaking during the downswing.

● Position the ball an inch inside the heel of the right foot for this shot. Your feet should be slightly less than a shoulder-width apart and your knees flexed.

● Depending on your strength and ability, a full swing with a pitching wedge will carry the ball about 100 yards. Adjust the power of the shot to position the ball accurately.

● Remember not to break your leading wrist as you approach the bottom of the swing. Rely on the angle of the clubface to give you the loft that you need.

● If you need to get the ball to loft quickly and land softly, try easing your grip with the last three fingers of the upper hand. This will cause the swing to speed up and give a quicker lift-off.

● Follow the shot through, keeping your eyes looking down at the impact spot until the momentum of the swing lifts your head naturally.

● The end of the swing sees your hips and shoulders turned in the direction of the target, with all your weight on the front foot.

▶ **downswing**   ▶ **impact**   **follow through**   ▶ **finish**   ■

sand wedge *approach shots*

The sand wedge will often be the loftiest club in your bag. Here's
how you use it for a lob of up to 90 yards.

● Stance is all-important with a lob
shot such as this. Position the ball in
line with your right heel. Your feet
should be less than shoulder-width
apart, with your leading foot an inch
behind.

● Before you start the swing, check
that your position is correct. You
should be looking down onto the ball,
your knees should be flexed and the
clubface should be pointing in the
direction of the target.

● Keep the weight on the balls of
your feet as you bring the club back.
This will give your arms much more
freedom to swing down onto the ball.

● At the top of the backswing, the
rear arm is guiding the club. The
leading arm remains nearly straight
throughout the swing.

● With the lob shots, there is less movement of weight between each side of the body. Keeping the weight more or less centred will create a steadier, more focused shot.

● At impact, the blade of the club slides under the ball, giving it both lift and backspin.

● Even though you want the ball to lift quickly, don't try to change the swing to make this happen. Hit down onto the ball as usual and this will make sure that the blade of the club does its job and lifts the ball for you.

● Turn through the shot and end the swing with your waist and shoulders facing the direction of the target.

▶ **downswing**   ▶ **impact**   **follow through**   ▶ **finish** ■

When you get close to the green, you want to move your ball gently and accurately towards the pin. The pitch and run gives the ball a short flight and a longer run along the green. Imagine you are throwing the ball underarm to estimate where to land it so that you end up near – or in – the hole.

● This is not a full swing, and your stance will need some adjustment. First of all, your feet should be closer together than with a full swing – about 12 inches between the heels.

● Bring your left foot back slightly to open up your stance. Your shoulders line up parallel with the line between your toes. Most of your weight (about 80 per cent) should be on the leading leg and your hands ahead of the ball.

● Place the ball just inside your right heel. Throughout this swing, you are going to keep your arms and shoulders in their triangle shape. The wrists and elbows should not break.

● Adjust the height of your swing according to the distance you need the ball to travel, but don't take it above the horizontal.

● Keep your weight settled on the leading foot throughout the swing. As you make contact, the hands are again ahead of the ball. This will help to guarantee a good, solid, downward impact with the ball.

● Keep your head down right to the end of the follow through. This shot has more in common with your putting stroke than a full swing.

● The follow through is still important in this diminutive swing. Keep your head down and let the arms swing up to the height of the backswing.

▶ **downswing**　　　　　▶ **impact**　　　　**follow through**　　　▶ **finish**　　■

sand wedge – pitch and run

The sand wedge can be used when you need more loft than you would get from a 7-iron, but still
need a bit of run-on. This shot will lift the ball more sharply than the 7-iron and the ball will land with
less forward momentum.

● For this shot, open your stance up
more than you would for the 7-iron
pitch and run. Bring the leading foot
back two inches and line your
shoulders up with your feet.

● Place the ball towards the back of
your stance, level with the heel of the
rear foot. The blade of the club should
face in the direction of the target.

● Swing the club using mainly your
hands, wrists, and arms. You will only
need minimal shoulder or waist
movement for this type of shot.

● Keep an even tempo throughout
the swing – try not to start too
quickly or too slowly. This will take
practise to get right.

● From this angle, we can see the open stance of the pitch more clearly. We can also see that the shoulders are also opened up.

● The arms and the hands swing, but the movement of the waist and shoulders is restrained.

● The power of the shot is measured by the height of the backswing. You can take the arms up to horizontal. Any more than this and your shot will probably end up over-shooting the green altogether.

● The shoulders and waist come into play as you play through the ball. Keep your head down throughout this shot.

■ set up ▶ takeaway   backswing ▶ downswing   impact   follow through   finish ■

putter

Putting any loft on the ball can be an unpredictable business. You might find yourself in a position where you can use a putter to get onto the green. This can be more accurate than a pitch shot, but is only possible on the short grass that surrounds the green – not from the fairway.

● Place the ball inside the heel of your leading foot. Look down onto the ball with your hands slightly forward of the ball.

● The movement of the swing starts (and remains) in the shoulders. The arms, wrists and hands stay passive throughout. Keep your head still.

● The backswing will be higher than for a normal putt on the green. The height will depend on the power you need, which in turn will depend on the contours of the ground between you and the hole.

● Keep the triangle formed by your hands, arms and shoulders intact throughout the swing. The action is basically a pendulum motion.

● The impact should connect the flat face of the putter with the ball, striking in the intended direction of the shot. The hands are slightly ahead of the clubhead when contact occurs.

● Keep the triangle intact and your head down as you follow through the swing. Lifting your head could cause you to hit the ball off-centre.

● The follow through should take the club up to a height equal to that of the backswing. Keep your head down until the shot is completely finished.

► **downswing**　　　► **impact**　　　**follow through**　　　► **finish** ■

awkward lies

uphill lies

An uphill lie causes some changes to your stance as well as where you aim your shot. The idea is to achieve a good, clean impact with the ball while adapting to the gradient of the fairway. Use a longer club than normal, since the slope will cause the ball to launch at a steeper angle.

● Stand with your feet slightly wider than shoulder width apart. Position the ball towards the front of your stance, in line with the heel of your front foot.

● Your shoulders should lie parallel with the gradient – use your knees to adjust to the slope and give you balance. They should be flexed slightly in an uphill direction.

● Keep most of your weight on the rear foot as you start the swing. Your front knee will bend in towards the ball as the backswing proceeds.

● As with a normal swing, the rear knee provides power for the shot, but, in this case, it also provides balance and stability.

● Once your downswing is beyond horizontal, the momentum of your upper body lets you shift weight onto the front leg, just as in a normal swing – and without losing your balance. The rear knee can now break.

● Continue to shift weight forward onto the leading foot as the club impacts with the ball. On an uphill lie, you should usually aim slightly to the right of the target.

● Follow through as usual, although you will probably find more weight than usual left on the rear side of the body. Try to keep your balance as you finish the swing.

▶ **downswing**   ▶ **impact**   **follow through**   ▶ **finish**   ■

downhill lies

For downhill lies, the same principles apply as with the uphill lie. The idea is to adapt your normal swing and stance to the new situation. Since the slope will cause the trajectory of your shot to be lower than usual, consider using a shorter club for extra loft.

● Position the ball towards the back of your stance. Your weight will naturally shift to the leading leg, try to keep about 40 per cent on the rear foot. Have your shoulders as parallel with the ground as is comfortable.

● As the backswing proceeds, you will find that your weight doesn't shift back to the rear foot as it normally would. In fact, it will probably become centred over the ball.

● Despite the lack of weight transfer, you should focus on getting your body turned as much as possible.

● In the downswing, concentrate on making a normal contact with the ball. Don't try to help the ball into the air to make up for the downhill slope.

● With the ball back in your stance, the clubface will be at a steeper angle than usual and the ball will be given more loft. Let the club do the work and don't try to lift the ball.

● Keep the club as low as possible immediately after impact, almost following the contours of the slope. This will help you to avoid trying to lift the ball artificially.

● It can be very easy to overbalance forwards in the follow through. Try to keep some weight on the rear foot, but without leaning backwards. Getting the weight transfer right for this shot will take some practice.

▶ **downswing**   ▶ **impact**   **follow through**   ▶ **finish** ■

ball above feet *lies*

When the ball is lying above your feet you can't use your normal stance. If you
stand at 90 degrees to the ground in this situation, you will fall backwards.

● As you address the ball make a few
adjustments to compensate for the
slope. You will have to lean into the
slope to keep your balance.

● Because you are leaning forwards,
you will be closer to the ball than
usual, so grip the club further down
the shaft to compensate. Position the
ball forwards in your stance.

● You should be able to keep the
transfer of weight running as usual.
Shift it onto your rear foot as you turn
the shoulders and waist back.

● Keep the rear knee flexed as you
reach the top of the backswing and
move into the downswing. Your weight
will start to transfer forwards onto the
leading side of your body.

● Keep the swing running as normal. Shift your weight onto the leading foot and start to pivot on your leading hip.

● At impact, your head should be behind the clubhead. Otherwise, continue to play the shot as normal.

● With awkward lies on slopes, keeping your balance in the follow through is crucial. First, because falling over is dangerous. Second, because instability in your stance will affect the impact with the ball.

● Don't carry the follow through on as far as usual, as this could send you tumbling down the slope.

downswing ▶ **impact** **follow through** ▶ **finish**

ball below feet

A ball that is lying below your feet can be one of the hardest lies to deal with. Your sense of balance

will be tested as you get the right line between leaning too far backwards and falling forwards.

● You will have to lean back to compensate for the slope. Grip your club towards the top of the shaft to lengthen the club – making up for the greater distance between your hands and the ball.

● Position the ball towards the back of your stance, with your hands forward of the ball. Use a slightly open stance, as there is a tendency for the ball to fade to the right. Aim to the left of the target.

● The weight transfer between the leading and rear side of the body shouldn't be too affected by the slope, unless it is a diagonal – in which case you need to combine this stance with those on the previous pages.

● Transfer weight onto the rear side of the body through the backswing, coiling your body ready for the downswing and impact with the ball.

  ǁ set up   ▶   **takeaway**   ▶   **backswing**

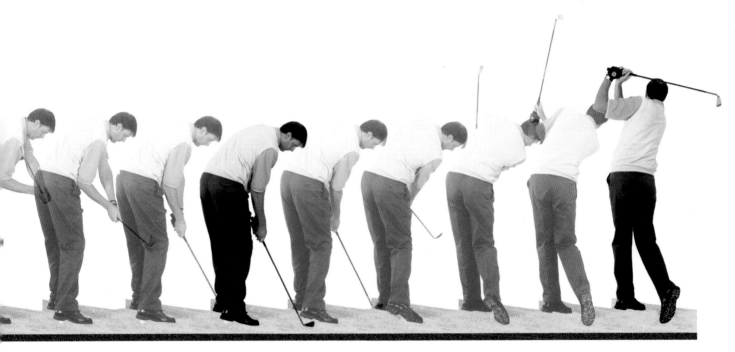

● Weight shifts forwards again on the downswing. This is when you will find out if you have balanced yourself properly.

● Your hands should be ahead of the ball at impact, just as they were when you were setting up the shot.

● Let your weight continue to pivot around on your leading hip. This action should keep you from falling forwards down the slope.

● The open stance you adopted at the set-up should help to keep your balance – use your rear foot as a support if you feel yourself leaning down the slope.

▶ **downswing**　　　　　▶ **impact**　　　　**follow through**　　　　▶ **finish**　■

long grass

All players, whatever standard, have to deal with long grass or rough. There are a number of factors you need to consider when playing from long grass. As well as the challenge of getting the ball out, you also have little control over the flight of the ball.

● When you set up your shot, hover the club an inch above and behind the ball. Moving the ball after the address means a one-shot penalty. If you don't ground the club, you haven't technically made your address.

● Position the ball back in your stance and grip the club an inch further down the shaft than normal. Use a shorter club than you would normally use for the distance.

● Keep your head above the ball through the backswing: you need to have a steep angle of attack for this shot to dig the ball out of the grass.

● Play down onto the ball, making sure you don't forget the essentials of your swing. Make it a strong downswing, otherwise the grass could alter the angle of the clubhead.

● The clubhead should punch down behind the ball. Let the changes to your stance make this happen. If you overcompensate, you could miss the ball altogether.

● As the ball is launched, it won't have any backspin. This is because the grass comes between the blade and the ball. Take this into account – the ball could shoot out too fast and run on for yards when it lands.

● If the lie is really bad, consider simply trying to hit the ball to a playable position. Better this than hacking your way through the rough.

▶ **downswing**　　　　　　▶ **impact**　　　　　**follow through**　　　　▶ **finish**　　■

divots *awkward lies*

Digging your ball out of a divot (a hole caused by a previous shot) requires a similar approach to that used when getting out of long grass. You need to adjust your set up and stance so that you can chop down onto the ball and launch it.

● Depending on the depth of the divot, choose a shorter club than you would normally use for this distance. The depth of the divot will stop the ball from lofting too much.

● Position the ball back in your stance and move your hands forwards of the ball. This will help you to chop down onto the ball at a steep enough angle.

● Make the backswing more upright, by pushing the arms away from the body as they swing back. Also, cock your wrists more than usual.

● Attack down onto the ball. Don't make the downswing too fast, though. The key is to get a good, solid impact, which you could miss if you try to hit the ball too hard.

● At impact, the blade should dig in behind the ball and carry on through. You'll be digging an even bigger hole. Depending on the angle of attack, the shot could end here.

● The trajectory of the ball will be lower than usual and will run on further when it lands, so take this into account.

● Unlike the person who made the original divot, be sure to replace any turf that you have dug out.

▶ **downswing** ▶ **impact** **follow through** ▶ **finish** ■

bunker play

fairway bunkers

Bunkers don't just lurk around the edge of the green. Sometimes a wayward tee shot can find a bunker on the edge of the fairway. You might still have over 200 yards to play, so simply lofting out of the bunker won't be enough. You are going to need to play a normal fairway shot from an unusual position.

● You will need at least some loft to get out of a bunker, so you should use no lower than a 5-iron for the job. If there is a serious lip to get over, you will need one of the greenside bunker techniques to get out.

● The temptation in the bunker is to try to dig the ball out with a serious downwards chop. As you still have some distance to go, this won't do. You'll need to scoop the ball out of the sand cleanly to make a good shot.

● Get a good, solid footing before you start. Remember not to ground the ball onto the sand before the shot itself – this will cost you a shot.

● Play a normal shot at the right angle of attack for the club. Playing from a bunker can at times be preferable to playing from the rough.

● At impact, the club should cut cleanly through the sand and make a good, solid contact with the ball. If you dig the club in too deep, you will lose the power of the shot.

● Follow through as normal, keeping your head down. A common tendency in bunkers is to lean back to get more loft – this will not help your shot here.

● As when playing out of rough, a ball played out of sand will not have much backspin and will run on further than usual. Remember to rake the sand before you walk up to your ball.

▶ **downswing**　　　　　▶ **impact**　　　　**follow through**　　　▶ **finish**　■

shallow bunker play

In this situation, you need to play as close to a normal chip shot as possible. You don't need to create extra elevation to clear the lip of the bunker. From this position, you can deliver a neat, controlled shot onto the green – without getting lost in a shower of sand.

● Adopt a square stance to the green. Keep the blade of the sand wedge square onto the ball as well, rather than the open face required for extra lofted clubs. Make sure that you have got a firm, even footing.

● Keep the ball in the centre of your stance. Do not ground the blade on the sand before the shot, as this will incur a penalty stroke. Address the club an inch behind the ball.

● Adjust the height of the backswing to suit the strength of shot required. Next to the green, this should rarely be much beyond the horizontal.

● On the downswing, you are aiming the club to hit two or three inches behind the ball.

● At impact, the club should scoop up the ball, together with the small area of sand around it.

● For this shot, the follow through is crucial – as it helps to make sure that the club has enough momentum to cut cleanly through the sand.

● As the club made little or no contact with the ball, there will be very little backspin – so allow for some run on after the ball lands.

deep bunker *play*

Some bunkers are designed to be extremely difficult to exit. They are constructed with high walls between you and the green, making a straightforward shot almost impossible. In this situation you will need to achieve a high trajectory to get your ball onto the green.

● Open your stance by pulling your left foot back. You will need to bring your foot back quite a way to achieve the correct stance. Placing your feet like this will allow you to lean your body away from the ball and gain a higher trajectory.

● Now open the blade of the sand wedge to the point where the face is looking straight up to the sky. The ball should be positioned slightly forwards, just behind the left heel. This is especially important if the ball is close to the face of the bunker.

● Your hands should be behind the ball. Although this stance might feel strange, the face of the club should be positioned in such a way that you feel you will slice right under the ball when you do the swing. This is what the sand wedge was designed for.

● Remember that your club must not touch the sand before you hit the ball, so be careful when you raise the club for the backswing, or you could incur a penalty.

● Aim to hit the sand about seven centimetres (two and half inches) behind the ball. Swing the club at roughly 80 per cent of your full speed.

● Don't hit downwards, but think of it as a sliding motion where you try to slide the clubhead under the ball. Focusing on a full follow through will help you achieve the correct shot.

● Let the clubhead throw a scoop of sand onto the green. The more sand you throw, the shorter the shot will be. If you need to hit the shot some distance, then hit closer in to the ball, perhaps just five centimetres (two inches).

▶ **downswing**   ▶ **impact**   **follow through**   ▶ **finish** ■

a plugged ball

Sometimes a golf ball can disappear into the sand of a bunker. Momentum simply drives the ball under the surface. This is known as a 'plugged lie' or, less formally, a 'fried egg'. Getting your ball out of this predicament without the use of heavy digging equipment requires a slightly different approach to normal bunker play.

● Choose your club. Sometimes a pitching wedge can be preferable to a sand wedge as they can have sharper leading edges for better 'digging'. Look down onto the ball and keep your knees well flexed.

● Position the ball towards the centre or a little to the rear of your stance. Play this shot square onto the ball, and not in the open stance of other bunker shots.

● At the address stage, hover the club an inch above and behind the ball, with the leading edge aiming at the base of the ball (you will have to estimate where this is). Remember not to touch the sand before the shot.

● Make a short backswing, bringing the clubface to point directly upwards. You are preparing to strike down just behind the ball.

● Bring the club down sharply a couple of inches behind the ball. The clubface should literally dig the ball out from its sandy grave.

● Because of the extreme downward angle of this shot, there is not much of a follow through after the shot – if any at all. If all goes to plan, the ball should pop out of the sand, onto the green.

● Because the club makes little if any contact with the ball, there will be no backspin and the ball will run on. Aim your shot well short of the pin.

▶ **downswing**   ▶ **impact**   **follow through**   ▶ **finish**   ■

on the green

the basic putting stroke

Putting is almost a game in its own right. You don't want to take any more than 36 putts per 18 holes, which is 2 putts per hole. If you can learn to putt in one, you can rapidly improve your handicap. The swing and grip are very different from any other stroke.

● To help you judge the distance of the putt, stand behind the ball and imagine it rolling towards the hole. This should help you to apply the right amount of strength when you putt the ball.

● For this shot, the movement is in the arms and shoulders. Keep your arms locked and maintain the triangle shape as you address the ball. Make sure your eyes are over the ball when you are in this position.

● As you take the clubhead back, concentrate on creating a pendulum action controlled predominantly by the shoulders, with your hands remaining passive. Keep your head still

● A rule for this stroke is not to let the clubhead pass your hands. To ensure this doesn't happen, place your leading hand in a line below the other, so the wrist is locked into position and remains firm through the ball.

● Although you should always aim to hole out with one putt, if you are performing a long putt then you can practise by aiming the ball close to the hole. Your objective is for your putt to finish just a tap away from the hole.

● Concentrate on trying to swing the putterhead through impact. Avoid a descending strike as this may result in the ball jumping into the air.

● Hold your follow through position and don't be tempted to look up too early. Keep your eyes on the green until the ball is on its way towards the hole.

| downswing | ▶ | impact | follow through | ▶ | finish | ■ |

putting downhill

Golf courses are not flat.
As they need to be drained,
greens will always have a high
and low point. Putting downhill
can be one of the most
challenging golf shots,
requiring judgement and skill.

● When judging the power of your shot aim to give the ball a light enough tap towards the yellow cross to curve it towards the hole. Depending on the gradient of the slope, gravity will compensate for the lack of power.

● Adopt a normal putting stance, with your heels in line with your shoulders, your eyes over the ball and your shoulders and arms forming a triangle.

● Your feet should be aligned along the line of your putt. Remember, if there is a side gradient, this target line may not be directly towards the hole.

● Make sure your backswing is appropriate to the power of the shot. Don't over hit the ball, or you are likely to miss the hole.

● Make the backswing and the downswing one entire, smooth movement, without pausing at the top of the backswing.

● At impact, the clubhead should hit directly through the ball. Remember to hit the ball just past the target. Resist the temptation to over-power your shot though.

● Complete the follow through to ensure that your swing is smooth and solid, without wavering or hesitation.

▶ **downswing**　　　　　▶ **impact**　　　　**follow through**　　　▶　**finish**　■

putting across a slope

Slopes, which are also referred to as a 'borrow', need to be taken into consideration when planning a swing. When putting across a slope it is usually best to aim off-line in order to compensate for the gradient. Here we outline the hanging-club technique for working out the amount of gradient, or borrow, on a particular green.

● Use the hanging shaft of your putter to find your target line. Stand behind the ball, in line with the hole. Hold the putter in front of you at arm's length and point the toe of the club in line with the ball and the hole. Aim for the yellow cross.

● Using the hanging shaft as a plumb-line, you will then be able to gauge the amount of borrow between the ball and the hole.

● Place the ball forward in your stance so that it is roughly opposite the inside of your left heel. Remember the golden rule that your eyes must be over the ball – this will determine the line that you want the ball to travel.

■   ‖ **set up**   ▶   **takeaway**   ▶   **backswing**

The length of your backswing is crucial. Make sure you don't take the club back too far and remember to aim along the target line you have calculated and not directly at the hole.

Depending on the gradient of the slope, you will need to strike the ball harder than when putting on a level course. Make the backswing and the downswing one entire, smooth movement, without pausing at the top of the backswing.

Avoid a descending strike as this may result in the ball jumping into the air. Concentrate on trying to swing the putterhead through impact. Remember to hit the ball just past the target.

Hold your follow-through position and keep your eyes on the green until the ball is on its way towards the hole.

▶ **downswing**　　　　　▶ **impact**　　　　**follow through**　　　▶ **finish**　■

speciality shots

The last thing you want when hitting into the wind is loft. The golden rule is to keep the ball low and get it down as quickly as possible. The most common mistake is to try to hit the ball harder – a smooth, tight swing is the key to this shot.

● Using a 1-iron, position the ball further back than the normal tee shot. This will help to keep the ball down. Also, position your hands ahead of the ball – this will also help to keep the shot low and avoid too much loft.

● As you take the club away from the ball, keep the clubhead as low as possible. Weight shifts from the leading leg onto the rear leg.

● This will be a three-quarter swing, so don't bring the arms as far back as you would for a normal tee shot.

● On the downswing, you will not sweep up through the ball as much as with a normal tee shot. Instead, this shot is more of a punch into the ball.

● At impact, the hands are ahead of the clubhead. This will cause the ball to lift off at a shallower angle.

● As the ball flies off, it will have less backspin than usual. This will also help to reduce the amount of loft. You should end up with a long, low trajectory that has a good run-on once it has landed.

● The follow through for this shot is not as extended as usual. This is because you are not trying to power against the wind, but instead punching the ball under it.

downswing ▶ **impact** **follow through** ▶ **finish** ◼

producing a draw

speciality shots

Sometimes, the layout of a hole or the lie of your ball means that you can't just hit a straight shot. Draw is the movement of the ball from right to left (for right-handers). This movement is created by putting draw spin onto the ball at impact. This in turn is done by changing your stance.

● When you set up the shot, face the clubface towards the target. The target is the line you are aiming for before the draw kicks in. This is the line that the first half of the shot will follow.

● With the club looking at the target line, move your leading foot forward. The amount you close your stance in this way depends on how much draw you wish to create.

● Tighten up the grip with your leading hand by turning it clockwise. In other words, so that more of your knuckles are visible than usual.

● At the top of the backswing, the club should be pointing to the right of the target line.

● At contact, the ball will leave in the target direction. However, the impact will have produced a lateral spin on the ball that causes it to move off the target line as it travels through the air.

● When the ball lands, the draw spin will cause it to run further than usual. Take this into account when choosing the club and power of the shot.

● Follow the shot through as usual, you may find yourself more coiled around your left hip than normal, due to the closed stance of the shot.

▶ **downswing**   ▶ **impact**   **follow through**   ▶ **finish** ◼

producing a fade

A fade is a shot which moves from left to right for a right-handed player. As with a draw, it is created by putting spin on the ball at impact. Again, the spin is created by changing the alignment of your stance as you address the ball.

● As with the draw shot, the secret of the fade is all in the stance. Aim the clubface in the direction of the target line. This will be the initial direction that the ball takes before it starts to fade from left to right.

● Swing the club along the line of your feet as you start the backswing. This will take the clubhead first out of the line of the shot.

● As the the swing reaches its peak, the club should be pointing to the left of the initial target direction. You can practise the shot using a mirror to check that this happens.

● Through the downswing, the club crosses from outside the line of the shot to inside the line.

● As the club strikes the ball, the clubhead is pointing in the target direction, but the club is actually moving to the left of the target line. This creates the correct spin to make the ball fade from left to right.

● The initial power of the impact will shoot the ball off in the target direction. As the ball loses momentum, it will start to fade left to right. So you can count on an initial straight flight with a late change.

● As you end the shot, you might find that your follow through is not as full as usual. Don't worry, this is a good sign as it means you have crossed the line of the target direction as you made your downswing.

▶ **downswing**   ▶ **impact**   **follow through**   ▶ **finish**   ■

producing a hook

A hook is a more extreme form of a draw. For many golfers, this type of shot is often produced by accident and can ruin their game. However, if you can produce a hook when you need it, it can become a useful part of your arsenal.

● To make the ball swing dramatically from right to left (to avoid an obstacle or to get round a sharp dog leg) first aim the club at the initial line that the ball will take before it starts to hook.

● Now bring your leading foot forwards. The amount depends on the strength of the hook you need. At least three inches forwards will do.

● Now start your backswing along the line of your feet. This will take the club inside the line of the target direction as the backswing progresses.

● Use a three-quarter swing for this shot. Reducing the power of the shot will allow the spin to take effect sooner and so the hook will be more pronounced. Hit too hard, and the ball with just draw rather than hook.

● Allow more movement in your wrists as your proceed through the downswing. The club should cross the target line from inside to outside in the last stages before impact.

● As the club strikes the ball it causes the ball to spin drastically. Combined with the reduced power of the shot, this will make the ball hook sharply from right to left.

● As with the draw, the ball will run on more than with a normal shot. Take this extra distance into account when choosing your club.

▶ **downswing**　　　　　▶ **impact**　　　　　**follow through**　　　　　▶ **finish**　　■

producing a slice *speciality shots*

A slice is an extreme form of fade. While a fade will only move from left to right late in the shot, the slice will start almost immediately to swing to the right. As with the hook, the slice is often a result of a poor swing, but can be harnessed to add a useful shot to your arsenal.

● Address the ball so that the clubface is aiming in the initial direction that the shot will take before the slice takes effect.

● Now move your leading foot back. The amount depends on how extreme you wish the slice to be. About three inches will produce a considerable slice.

● As you take the club away, start the backswing along the line of your feet. This will take the club out of the target line at first.

● As with the hook, the backswing for the slice is shorter than usual. This will mean that the spin takes effect sooner and the ball will move from left to right sooner in its trajectory.

● The downswing brings the club down across the line of the initial target direction from outside to the inside. The clubface will be pointing in the direction of the initial target line.

● As the club strikes the ball, the plane of the swing causes the ball to spin. Combined with the reduced power of the shot, the spin will cause the ball to move from left to right almost as soon as it gets in the air.

● Now that you've mastered this technique, practise will enable you to judge the amount of slice your stance will give to the ball.

▶ **downswing**   ▶ **impact**   **follow through**   ▶ **finish** ■

clearing tall obstacles

If you decide you need to go over an obstacle and not around it, some simple changes to your swing will help you achieve more loft, more quickly. This technique can be used to add height to any club.

● First, position the ball forward in your stance. Move your hands back from the target so that they are above the clubhead. This steep angle will maximize the loft of the club.

● You also need to lean back slightly to add to the loft effect. Achieve this by shifting more weight (about 60 per cent) onto the rear foot.

● Bring the club up at a steep angle. You are preparing to chop down onto the ball. At the top of the swing the club is pointing in the target direction.

● As the downswing proceeds, keep more weight than usual on your rear foot. This will help you to lean back into the impact stage of the swing.

● As you hit the ball, your hands should be in the same position as they were at the address (over the clubhead and the ball). This will give the ball greater loft.

● In the follow through try to keep your head and shoulders leaning back away from the target.

● Keep leaning back as you complete the shot. This will enable you to give the ball maximum lift at impact.

▶ **downswing**　　　　　　▶ **impact**　　　　　　**follow through**　　　　▶ **finish**　■

spotting common problems

spotting a hook problems

The persistent hook is not as
common as the slice,
however, it can still ruin your
game. As with the slice, the
main problem lies with the
shape of your swing – cutting
across the line from inside
to outside. A closed clubface
at impact also contributes
to the problem.

● The hook often starts with the
leading foot slightly forwards of the
target line.

● To compensate for the closed
stance, the face of the club is also
slightly closed.

● On the backswing, the club is
pushed out by the arms and ends up
too far back behind the body. The
shoulders do not turn enough.

■　　　　　　　　　　II set up　　　　▶　　　takeaway　　　▶　　　backswing

● Starting the downswing from this position, the club is attacking the ball from far too sharp an angle.

● The club hits the ball moving across the target line, swinging from inside to outside the line. Meanwhile, the face of the club is closed.

● The ball at first veers out to the right (for right-handed players). However, the angle at which the face of the club struck the ball soon causes it to hook back to the left.

● The hook shot ends with the club upright, pointing at the sky. The body has leaned over to the right.

spotting a slice

spotting problems

Slicing the ball is probably the most common fault of golfers. It is caused by a swing that crosses the target direction from the outside to the inside, sometimes made worse by an open clubface. The ball starts spinning on impact and soon moves from left to right in the air and away from the target.

● The slice usually starts with the leading foot back from the target line and the stance open. The face of the club can also end up open.

● At the takeaway, the club starts off travelling out of the target line. It is moving away from the body.

● The swing continues its wayward course, travelling away from the body. The top of the backswing sees the club pointing too high.

● On the downswing, the club once again moves outside the target line. The player is reaching too far over to compensate for his faulty posture.

● At impact, the club strikes the ball travelling across the target line from out to in. The face is still opened up.

● The combination of open face and out-to-in swing sends the ball at first veering to the left (for right-handed players) and then slicing to the right.

● The player ends up leaning over to the right, his arms extended and the club pointing up at the sky.

▶ **downswing**   ▶ **impact**   **follow through**   ▶ **finish**   ■

spotting a shank/in-to-out

In this sequence, we demonstrate the cause of one of the most

wayward shots in golf – the dreaded shank.

● The primary definition of a shank is when the ball is struck by the neck of the shaft, not the face of the club. The result is that the ball shoots off at an extreme angle left or right.

● Golf pros have identified 13 possible causes for the shank. Here, we demonstrate the most common of these – the locked waist syndrome. Standing too close to the ball can also be a common cause of shanking.

● As the backswing progresses, the waist is not turning. This forces the arms up into a position that is far too upright at the top of the backswing.

● As the downswing starts, the waist has not turned fully to face away from the target. This means that there is not enough body rotation. The arms are forced into a steep angle for the downswing, coming close to the legs.

● As the club approaches the ball, the
face has not turned to face the ball,
and the line of the swing is running
across the line of the target – from
inside to outside the line.

● At impact, the shaft of the club hits
the ball first. Where the ball ends up is
anyone's guess. Shanks have been
known to endanger spectators
standing alongside the player.

● In the follow through, the club will
continue to swing out, away from the
line of the target. Other than the
direction the ball takes, this can be the
most obvious symptom of a shank.

● The final position within the shank
can look like that of a normal shot –
leading to surprised looks at the
standard of the shot.

spotting a shank/out-to-in

In an out-to-in shank, the club swings at the ball from outside the target line. Like the in-to-out shank, this shot can be caused by standing too close to the ball. Here, we demonstrate the other common cause, moving the shoulders too early.

● Like the in-to-out shank, the out-to-in results in the shaft of the club striking the ball before the clubface.

● At the takeaway, the shoulders move away first, leaving the arms and the waist behind.

● At the top of the backswing, the shoulders again start turning before the arms and the waist. This pushes the elbows up and the club out.

● As the downswing progresses, the arms and club are still pushed out, trailing behind the shoulders.

● The club is now approaching the ball from well outside the target line. The elbows are coming close in to the body, grazing the hips.

● At impact, the shaft of the club hits the ball first. The shot can sometimes end at this point, as the elbows, club or both collide with the thighs.

● The club swings out behind the player. Instead of a neat arc, the swing has taken the shape of a messy spiral.

▶ **downswing**   ▶ **impact**   **follow through**   ▶ **finish**   ■

spotting a pull

A pull is a less extreme version of an out-to-in shank. The club ends up approaching the ball from outside the target line and the resulting shot veers off to the left (for right-handed players).

● Like the out-to-in shank, the pull usually results from moving the shoulders too early. The swing often begins looking quite normal.

● On the backswing, the shoulders and chest are slightly ahead of the arms and waist. At this point, the shot still does not look too bad.

● At the top of the backswing, the shoulders and chest are still ahead of the arms. They start into the downswing before the arms have finished the backswing.

■   ‖ set up   ▶   takeaway   ▶   backswing

● The shoulders continue to lead, while the arms and club trail behind. The elbows remain broken.

● The club is now out of the proper plane of the swing, approaching the ball from outside the target line.

● At impact, the club strikes across the ball. It strikes the ball in completely the wrong direction. Spectators down the fairway need to take cover.

● The club continues its wayward journey, swinging out behind the player. Playing bad shots like this repeatedly can be seriously bad for your spine – and score card.

▶ **downswing**   ▶ **impact**   **follow through**   ▶ **finish** ■

spotting a push

The push is the little cousin of
the in-to-out shank. Like its
senior relation, the push has
the club swinging at the ball
from inside the target line –
sending the ball to the right
(for right-handers).

● Like the in-to-out shank, the push
usually results from not enough
movement in the waist for the swing.

● The waist is not turning enough to
the rear during the backswing. This
throws the whole of the rest of the
body out of alignment.

● The arms are forced into a very
steep angle at the top of the
backswing, compensating for
the lack of waist movement.

● The downswing has the club travelling from inside to outside the line. The clubface is in line with the ball, if the clubface was closed you would end up with a hook.

● At impact, the ball is fired off to the right (for a right-handed player). Unlike a hook, which starts right and swerves to the left, the push starts right and stays right.

● During the follow through, the club continues to swing out, and the player may lean forward or even overbalance.

● You will notice that the arms are more upright through the follow of the swing.

▶ **downswing**   ▶ **impact**   **follow through**   ▶ **finish** ■

spotting a topped shot

Topping the ball means hitting it above the centre, so that instead of flying up, it is driven down by the bottom of the club. It can be the most humiliating and frustrating of all bad shots.

● A topped shot can be caused by simply placing the ball too far forward in your stance for the club. This will mean that the club is already swinging up when it reaches the ball. So check ball position carefully.

● Another cause of topping is leaning back too much in the set up. Make sure your weight is on the balls of the feet, not the heels.

● Raising the head during the backswing is probably the most common cause of topping. This removes the stabilizing effect of the head and allows the arms to rise up.

● Whatever the combination of elements that cause it, the downswing will result in the club either reaching the bottom of the swing too early, or flying out at too flat a plane.

● At impact, the clubhead strikes the top half of the ball. Depending on the exact latitude at which the club strikes, the ball could fly out flat, without elevation, or be driven straight into the ground, making no distance.

● During the follow through, it is common to overbalance as the club fails to make proper contact with the ball. You can also strain a muscle.

● Ending the shot properly is already forgotten as the plight of the unfortunate golf ball is clear to all.

▶ **downswing**   ▶ **impact**   **follow through**   ▶ **finish** ■

43321